MONSTER TAMER GIRLS 1
MUJIRUSHI SHIMAZAKI

CONTENTS

IT'S ALL RIGHT.
DON'T BE AFRAID.

CHAPTER ONE THE SCHOOL MONSTER

I'M...
職員室
SIGN: FACULTY OFFICE
...ION HIDAKA FROM... CLASS 1-T.
AND I'M SORA MISUMARU FROM 1-A.

HIDAKA...
...YOU'RE IN THE TAMERS PROGRAM, RIGHT?

OH... YES.
THEN I'M SURE YOU'RE ALREADY WELL AWARE, BUT...

...OUR SCHOOL, TATARA GIRLS' ACADEMY...
...IS WELL-KNOWN FOR ITS MONSTER DOMESTICATION... ER, TAMING CURRICULUM.
IT'S THE JOB OF THE TAMERS COMMITTEE MEMBERS TO CARE FOR THE MONSTERS SENT HERE EVERY SO OFTEN FOR HANDS-ON PRACTICE...

...BUT THERE'S ONE THAT'S BEEN LIVING IN THE FOREST BEHIND THE SCHOOL FOR YEARS NOW.
GASA (RUSTLE)
IN ANY CASE, IT'S THE FIRST-YEARS' JOB TO TAKE CARE OF THIS ONE.

SO...PLAY
NICE WITH
EACH
OTHER.

ギロ
GIRO (GLARE)

ひっ
EEK!

ANYTHING YOU NEED IS OVER IN THAT EQUIP-MENT SHED.
CONSULT THE TAMERS' MANUAL FOR MORE INFO.
OHH!
HUH ...?
BUT ...

ぷい
PUI (SNUB)

ズン
ZUN (THUD)

WOW, SEEING IT UP CLOSE, IT IS PRETTY IMPRES-SIVE.

ION?

... THAT'S WHAT I'M CALLING YOU.
YOU CAN CALL ME SORA.
O-OKAY.

SORA...CHAN, YOU'RE IN GEN ED, SO WHY ARE YOU ON THE TAMERS COMMITTEE...?
I FAILED THE APTITUDE TEST FOR THE TAMERS PROGRAM!!
OH... S... SORRY ...

BUT I LOVE MON-STERS.
YOU DO TOO, DON'T YOU, ION?

UM... I...
OH, THERE IT IS.

I GUESS... IT'S SLEEPING?

LET'S SEE.
"MONSTERS' BODIES PRODUCE NUTRIENTS VIA A PROCESS SIMILAR TO PHOTO-SYNTHESIS AND THUS DO NOT EAT ANYTHING.
"IN EXCHANGE, THEY REGULARLY REQUIRE CLEAN WATER."
BOOK: —COMMITTEE—

IT SAYS WE NEED TO CHANGE THE DRINKING WATER IN ITS TANK ONCE A MONTH.
DO YOU KNOW WHAT THE BOOK'S TALKING ABOUT, ION?

UH... M...
OH.

SIGN: EQUIPMENT SHED
用具庫
MAYBE THAT'S... IT...?
IT'S KIND OF LIKE WHAT A HAMSTER DRINKS WATER FROM...
THAT'S IT!
JUST WHAT I'D EXPECT FROM A TAMER-TO-BE!
IT'S NOT THAT...
THERE'S SOMETHING LIKE A SWITCH.
LET'S GET A STEP-LADDER.
...HEY, SORA-CHAN.
IF WE OPEN THIS UP FURTHER, THE LADDER WILL GET TALLER...
JUST A LITTLE FARTHER!
HOLD MY LEGS STEADY.
GACHA (KACHAK)
ガチャッ
給 FEED
排 DRAIN

ぼすん
BOSUN (FLOP)
HUH?
AH...

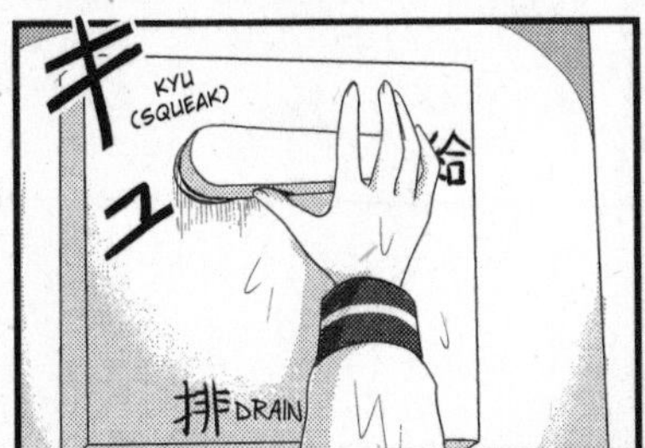

SIGN: EQUIPMENT SHED

AWW-RIGHT, NOW THAT WE'VE GOTTEN CLEANED UP...
1-A
1-T 日高
...LET'S RINSE IT OFF AND GET IT CLEAN.
ごっし
GOSSHI (SCRUB)
ごっし
GOSSHI
ごし
GOSHI
ごし
GOSHI
ごし…
GOSHI
ごし…
GOSHI
SHIRTS: 1-A SORA MISUMARU / 1-T ION HIDAKA
PHEW...
ALL THAT TIME AND WE'VE ONLY DONE HALF THE FACE...

ズーン
ZUN (THUD)
HUH?
WHERE IS IT GOING?

OH YEAH, HAVING A WALK AROUND THE SCHOOL GROUNDS IS PART OF ITS DAILY ROUTINE.
UP WE GO.
IT SURE GOES AT ITS OWN PACE.

SORA-CHAN!
WAI—
1-T HID-

ずべ
ZUBE (SLIDE)

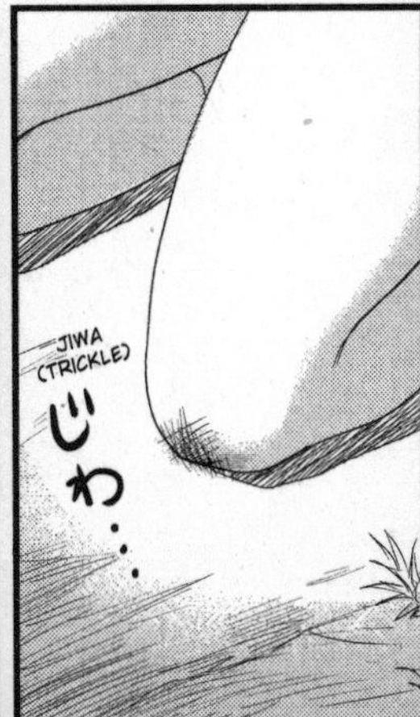
JIWA (TRICKLE)
じわ…

ぼろ
BORO (PLIP)
ぼろ
BORO

I...
...CAN'T TAKE ANYMORE...
1-T
日高唯音
SHIRT: 1-T ION HIDAKA
I ACTUALLY...
...DON'T LIKE MONSTERS.
I CAME HERE BECAUSE EVERYONE SAID I HAD A KNACK FOR IT.
I ENDED UP ON THE TAMERS COMMITTEE...
...BECAUSE I WAS LATE, AND BY THE TIME I GOT TO MY CLASSROOM, IT HAD ALREADY BEEN DECIDED...

えぐ
EGU (SOB)
えぐ
EGU
ぬ
NU (LOOM)
I THINK ...
...IT'S SAYING, "GET ON."

ZUN (THUD)
ZUN
WE'RE UP SO HIGH!
1-T 日高唯音
I CAN SEE THE OLD PART OF TOWN REALLY WELL.

THAT AREA WAS A HUGE SHOPPING DISTRICT BEFORE WE WERE BORN, RIGHT?
YUP.
I HEARD A LOT OF PEOPLE LIVED THERE.

SO ARE YOU...
...STILL AFRAID OF MON-STERS?

I'M NOT SURE.
BUT...
1-T

THAT'S WHEN...

...THIS OLDER TAMER GIRL APPEARED.

SHE SAID, "IT'S OKAY, DON'T BE AFRAID."

BUT SHE SAID IT *TO THE MONSTER*.

SHIRT: 1-A SORA MISUMARU

1-A

IT WAS...
...SO INCREDIBLY COOL.

AND THEN SHE SANG TO IT LIKE SHE WAS SOOTHING A BABY.
THE MONSTER QUICKLY CALMED DOWN.

I'VE ALWAYS WANTED TO BE LIKE HER.

I WONDER ...
...WHY I FORGOT.

HEY.
SINGING IS HOW TAMERS COMMUNI-CATE WITH MONSTERS, RIGHT?
YOU SHOULD TRY SINGING, ION.

N-N-N-N-NO WAY, I C-C-CAN'T.
I'VE NEVER, EVER SUNG IN FRONT OF ANYONE BEFORE...

IT'S OKAY.
IT'S JUST ME AND THIS ONE HERE!
THAT STILL DOESN'T MAKE IT OKAAAY!

CHERRY BLOS-SOMS ...?

THE SCHOOL COURT-YARD'S CHERRY BLOS-SOMS ...
...HAVEN'T BLOOMED IN YEARS ...

COULD IT BE...
...A BIO-TORRENT ...?

THIS IS ACTUALLY MY FIRST TIME SEEING IT.
WOW...

ZZZZ...

WELL THIS CERTAINLY IS RARE.
DO YOU LIKE THEM?

I SEE...
I'M GLAD.

I'M LEAVING YOU TWO TO IT...
...MY COMMITTEE MEMBERS.

1-A
御統宙

THAT IS THE ROLE FOR WHICH YOU ALL STRIVE—"TAMER"...

CHAPTER TWO THE MONSTER GRAVEYARD

AH HA HA HA HA!
COME ON, IT'S NOT FUNNY, SORA-CHAN!
AND IT WAS SUCH A PAIN, TAKING IT BACK TO THE FOREST.
IT MUST REALLY LIKE YOU, ION.
IT'S LIKE SUGITA-SENSEI SAID.
EVERY YEAR, THEY TAKE A SHOT AND HAVE THE FIRST-YEARS CARE FOR IT, BUT HAVING IT ACTUALLY WARM UP TO THEM IS RARE.
THAT'S "WARMING UP"...?
I, ION HIDAKA...
...AND THIS GIRL, SORA MISUMARU-CHAN...
...ARE MONSTER TAMERS.

WE'VE BEEN LEFT IN CHARGE OF CARING FOR A MONSTER WHO LIVES IN THE FOREST BEHIND THE SCHOOL.

BUT IT WON'T LISTEN TO WHAT WE SAY, SO THINGS ARE ROUGH.

SIGN: FACULTY OFFICE

OH...
DO YOU KNOW HER?

She's the chair of the Monster Tamers Committee! Sora-chan, you must've met her.
Ahh, she is?

YOU'RE THE FIRST-YEARS, HIDAKA-SAN AND MISUMARU-SAN.

Y-YES!

I'M TSUKIKO MIYAMA, A SECOND-YEAR.
IF THERE'S ANYTHING YOU DON'T UNDER-STAND ABOUT YOUR TAMERS COMMITTEE DUTIES, PLEASE ASK ME.

ALL RIGHT, THEN. LOOK FORWARD TO WORKING WITH YOU...
R... RIGHT ...
...?

SHE SEEMS KINDA SCARY.
YEAH... MAYBE.

WE'RE GOING TO...
...TAKE THE MONSTER OUT...?

YES.
ONE OF THE UNIVERSITY GRAD STUDENTS ...
...SAID SHE HAS SOME DATA SHE'D LIKE TO COLLECT.

THE RESEARCH LAB AFFILIATED WITH THE UNIVERSITY IS ALL THE WAY ON THE OTHER SIDE OF THE MOUNTAIN.
I'M COUNTING ON YOU GIRLS.

ROGER!
WHAAAT? THERE'S NO WAY, SORA-CHAN!
JUST TAKING IT FOR A WALK AROUND THE SCHOOL GROUNDS WAS A CHALLENGE...
OH, AND THE COMMITTEE CHAIR MIYAMA WILL ACCOMPANY YOU.

!!

O-OKAY, LET'S GET GOING, BLUE!
"BLUE"?
IT'S A BIT FLASHY FOR A NAME, DON'T YOU THINK?
I-I'M SORRY...
I HAD JUST HEARD THAT IT DIDN'T HAVE A NAME...

IT'S NOT THAT IT DOESN'T HAVE A NAME.
IT'S THAT NONE OF THEM HAVE STUCK.
JUST WITHIN MEMORY, THERE'S BEEN, "GONSUKE," "JUMBODON," AND "MOUNTAIN GORI."

I-I DON'T THINK I WOULD WANNA BE CALLED ANY OF THOSE NAMES...
ESPECIALLY NOT "MOUNTAIN GORI."
ZUN (THUD)
I CAME UP WITH THAT ONE.
I THOUGHT IT WAS A PERFECT FIT...

IT'S FOLLOWING US SO OBEDIENTLY.
I GUESS THAT'S UNUSUAL FOR IT...
I'M SURE IT ENJOYS GETTING OUT.
BY THE WAY, HIDAKA-SAN...
WHY DID YOU NAME IT "BLUE"?
OH... WELL ...
...THE COLOR OF ITS EYES IS MARINE-BLUE...
...AND THEY'RE REALLY PRETTY, SO...
YOU'RE RATHER STRANGE.
HUH ...?

USUALLY, WHEN YOU FACE SOMETHING LIKE IT...
...YOU WOULD NOTICE THE MASSIVE BODY OR THOSE GIANT HORNS FIRST, NOT ITS EYES.
I-I SUPPOSE SO...

IF YOU'RE THE COMMIT-TEE CHAIR-LADY, YOU MUST REALLY LIKE MON-STERS.
NOT ESPE-CIALLY.

I WON-DER...
...IF THAT'S WHY IT'S TAKEN TO YOU.

OKAY, REALLY NOT A FAN OF THIS CHICK.
I'M JUST...
...CURIOUS ABOUT THEM IS ALL.

LIKE ABOUT WHY THEY APPEARED HERE ON EARTH...
...OR WHETHER OR NOT IT'S REALLY POSSIBLE FOR HUMANS TO COEXIST WITH THEM.
HUH? BLUE...?

ZUN (THUD)
ズン
WAIT, WHERE ARE YOU GOING?
THAT'S NOT THE RIGHT WAY.

ぼすん
BOSUN (FLOP)
?
?
ぐらっ
GURA (WOBBLE)
EYAAAAAAGH!
ZUN (THUD)

HEY, NO FAIR!
LET ME RIDE TOO!
LET'S GO AFTER THEM!
AH... R-RIGHT.
WAAAIT!
ZUN
ズンッ

THIS IS LESS LIKE IT'S WARMING UP TO ME...

...AND MORE LIKE IT SEES ME AS A PERFECT-SIZED TOY.

LIKE THIS

ZUN (THUD)

IT GOT WIDE-OPEN ALL OF A SUDDEN...

ずずず
ZUZUZU (SSSLIDE)
ドサ
DOSA (FLOP)
WHERE IS THIS ...?

ROCKS ...?

BIG ONES TOO.

A SPOT WITH A GREAT VIEW, ALONG WITH A TON OF LARGE ROCKS...

THIS IS KIND OF LIKE—

A GRAVE-YARD.

IT'S NOT YET A WELL-KNOWN FACT, BUT...

...WHEN MONSTERS DIE, THEY BECOME STONES.

UH... UM...

THEN ALL OF THESE ARE...?
YES.
THEY WERE ALL ONCE MON-STERS.
THEY WERE MOVED HERE SO THAT THE UNIVERSITY COULD STUDY THEM.

KOTO ...?

TSUKIKO.

I'VE BEEN WAITING FOR YOU.
I KNEW IT HAD TO BE YOU, ASKING FOR ME BY NAME.

WELL, I'VE BEEN WANTING TO SEE YOU.

WE LIVE IN THE SAME DORM. WE CAN SEE EACH OTHER ANYTIME.

U-UM...

THIS IS KOTOMI JUSTINE KAGURA-ZAKA.

WE'RE THE SAME AGE, BUT SHE JUMPED AHEAD SEVERAL GRADES AND IS NOW IN THE GRADUATE PROGRAM.

I DID WANT TO GO TO MIDDLE SCHOOL WITH TSUKIKO, THOUGH.

ABOUT TEN YEARS AGO... BEFORE THIS LAB WAS BUILT HERE...
...THERE WAS A BIG FIRE ON THE MOUNTAIN.
THE WIND BLEW IT TOWARD THE CLIFF, SO THAT'S WHERE THE FIRE STOPPED SPREADING, BUT...
...THIS WHOLE AREA WAS COMPLETELY BURNED UP.

THAT STONE WAS FOUND AFTER THE FIRE.

THE ANIMALS TRAPPED AT THE EDGE OF THE CLIFF TOOK SHELTER BENEATH IT.

THEN THAT MONSTER WAS TRYING TO PROTECT THE ANIMALS...?

WE DON'T REALLY KNOW.

AS IF GUIDED BY SOMETHING...

...I SUDDENLY BEGAN TO SING.

THANKS TO YOU, WE WERE ABLE TO COLLECT SOME INTRIGUING DATA.
HEY, CHAIR-LADY!
DON'T YOU WANNA RIDE WITH US?
USING IT AS A TAXI SERVICE?
YOUR MEMBERS SURE ARE AMAZING.
JI (STARE)
じ…
はっ
HA (GASP)
I-I'M FINE, THANK YOU!
LET'S HURRY UP AND HEAD BACK!

A MONSTER GRAVE-YARD, EH...?
WHAT A MYSTE-RIOUS PLACE.

STILL, THAT STONE ...
WHEN I FIRST SAW IT, I THOUGHT IT WAS A MONSTER EGG.

WOULDN'T IT BE WONDERFUL IF ALL OF THOSE STONES HATCHED INTO MONSTERS !?
ズ
ZUN (THUD)
AH HA HA!
WON-DER... FUL...?

PISHI (CRACK)

CHAPTER THREE TSUKIKO'S DAY OFF

GORI!

MOUNTAIN GORI!

CHI (CHEEP) CHI
チチ…
CHI CHI CHI
チチチ

......
BLUE ...?

FIGURES THAT YOU'D PREFER THE NAME THOSE NEWBIES GAVE YOU.
WHAT-EVER.

IF YOU THINK IT FITS YOUR SELF-IMAGE BETTER, THEN I'LL GO ALONG WITH IT.
BUT GOING FOR THE NAME "BLUE" BECAUSE IT'S THE COLOR OF YOUR EYES?
THAT'S UNUSU-ALLY NARCIS-SISTIC OF YOU.

I'LL JUST GET TO THE POINT.
LET ME RIDE ON YOUR SNOUT.

YOU READILY LET THOSE NEWBIES HIDAKA-SAN AND MISUMARU-SAN RIDE ALONG WHILE YOU WALK ABOUT.
AS THE CHAIR OF THE TAMERS COMMITTEE, I NEED TO ENSURE THE SAFETY OF SUCH ACTIVITIES.
WHEEEE!
I SUPPOSE I'LL NEED TO HANDLE THIS LIKE A TAMER AND COMMUNICATE THROUGH SONG.
AHEM!
THERE IS NO OTHER WAY.
Oh, Blue...
...won't you please...
...let me ride on that snout of yours?

HUH? CHAIRLADY ...?

IT'S NOT THAT I, TSUKIKO MIYAMA...
...HATE MONSTERS OR ANY-THING.
AFTER ALL, I DID ENTER TATARA GIRLS' ACADEMY HERE WITH THE INTENT OF BECOMING A TAMER.
IF IT'S ONE OR THE OTHER, THEN I WOULD SAY I LIKE THEM.
IT'S JUST...
GASA (RUSTLE)
...THEY DON'T SEEM TO LIKE ME.
LIKE THAT HUGE MONSTER THAT LIVES IN THE FOREST BEHIND THE SCHOOL...
IT'S IN-FAMOUS FOR BEING HARD TO HANDLE...
...YET IT READILY EMBRACED THOSE TWO ROOKIES, HIDAKA-SAN AND MISUMARU-SAN.
THEY'RE SO LUCKY...

SIGN: TATARA GIRLS' ACADEMY DORM #1

多々来女学園
第一学生寮

TSU-KIKO.

WHY ARE YOU STARING OFF INTO SPACE LIKE THAT?

LIVING IN A DORM UP IN THE MOUNTAINS, SNACKS ARE A RARE TREAT!
AND THEN THERE'S THE WAY YOU OPEN THEM! I DON'T KNOW HOW MANY TIMES I'VE TOLD YOU...
OH COME ON.
ANYWAY, WHAT WE REALLY NEED TO TALK ABOUT IS OUR DATE TO-MORROW.

IT'S NOT A DATE, IT'S JUST A SHOP-PING TRIP.
PICK YOUR WORDS MORE CARE-FULLY.

MEANIE!
YOU'RE STUCK IN MIDDLE SCHOOL, SO I ONLY EVER GET TO HANG OUT WITH YOU ON THE WEEKENDS.

IT'S ONLY NATURAL FOR A MIDDLE SCHOOLER TO ATTEND MIDDLE SCHOOL.
YOU'RE THE ODD ONE. LEAPING AHEAD SEVERAL GRADES INTO GRADUATE SCHOOL ISN'T NORMAL, KOTO.

OH, I'LL SLEEP OVER TONIGHT.
YOU REALLY ARE A FREE SPIRIT, AREN'T YOU?

KOTO, WHAT ARE YOU DOING!!?

THE BUS IS GOING TO LEAVE US!!

WAIT UP!

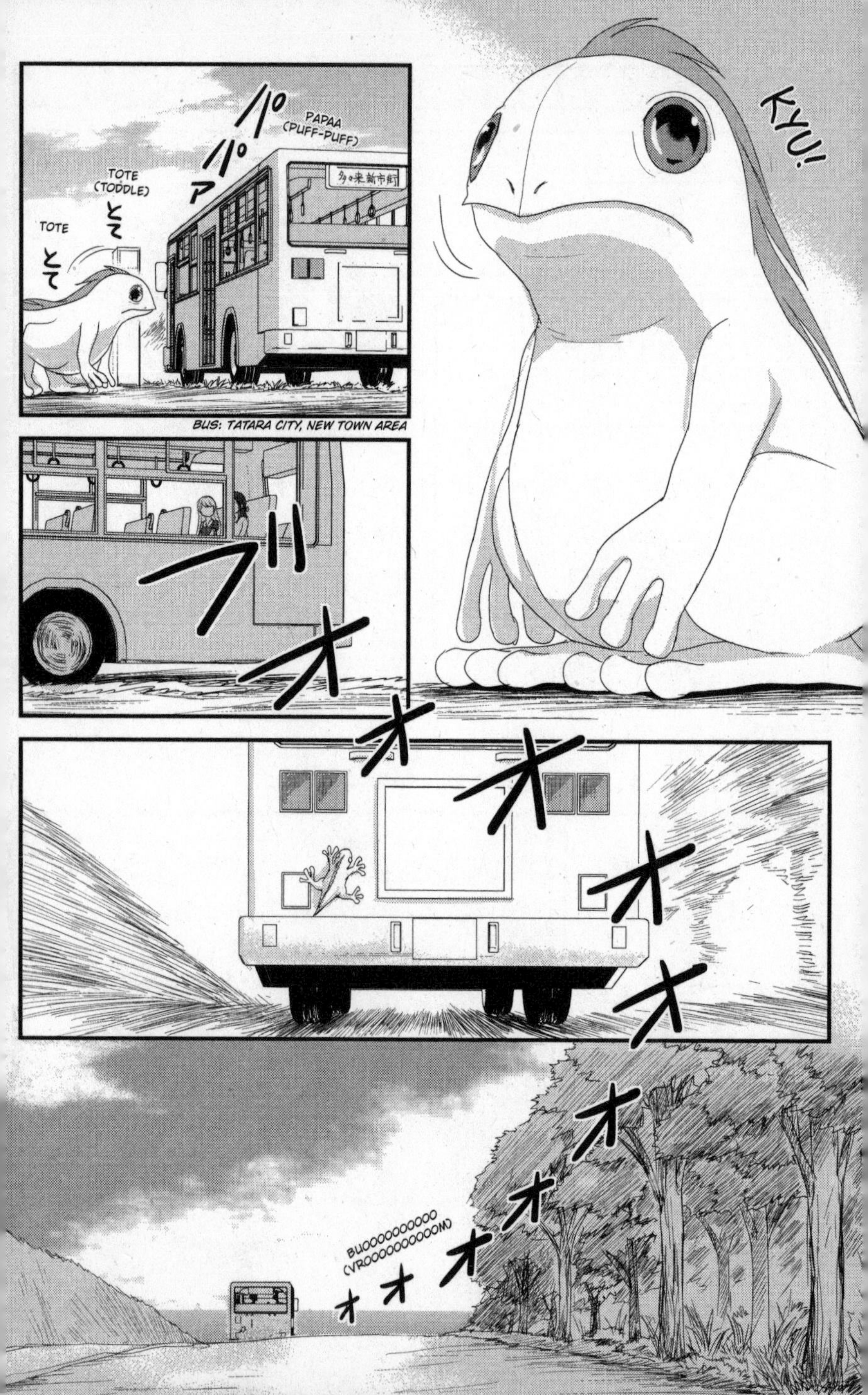
KYU!
パパァ
PAPAA (PUFF-PUFF)
多々来新市街
とて
TOTE (TODDLE)
とて
TOTE
BUS: TATARA CITY, NEW TOWN AREA
BUOOOOOOOOOO (VROOOOOOOOOOOM)

TSU-KIKO!

LET'S GET SOME ICE CREAM!

SURE.

WE'RE ALL DONE WITH SHOPPING, SO WE CAN TAKE A LITTLE BREAK.

YAY!

KOTO.

CAN YOU PLEASE HOLD THIS FOR ME WHILE I FIX MY SHOE-LACES?

AND DON'T EAT IT.

KAPU (OM)

かぷ

MOSHA (CRUNCH)
もしゃ
MOSHA
もしゃ
YOU LITTLE ...!
I WAS GONNA GET HALF OF THAT CHOCO MINT!
むに～～
MUNIIII (STREEETCH)
THAT WAS NEVER THE PLAN.
WAIT, MORE IMPOR-TANTLY ...

ぴょーーーん
PYOOON (BOING)
ぴと
PITO (CLING)
KYU!
きゅーーーん
KYUUUN (SWOON)

A-A MON-STER ...?
LOOKS THAT WAY.

IS IT A BABY ...?
CAN'T SAY.
SOME MONSTERS NEVER GET VERY BIG.

THE SPECIAL MONSTER SHELTER DISTRICT IN THE OLD PART OF TOWN IS NEARBY.
MAYBE IT ESCAPED FROM THERE.

I THOUGHT MONSTERS DIDN'T NEED TO EAT...?
WE NEED TO DO SOMETHING BEFORE THERE'S A COMMOTION.

MON ...

GYU (SHOVE)
ぎゅ

MEOW~~~
KOU-CHAAAN!

MEOOOW!

IT'S ALL RIGHT NOW.
KYU!

IT'S NOT VERY CUTE.
TH-THAT'S NOT TRUE AT ALL!

I'M SUR-PRISED.
HERE I THOUGHT YOU ONLY HAD A SCHOLARLY INTEREST IN MONSTERS, TSUKIKO.

AH... WELL, I MEAN...

...THEY DON'T SEEM TO LIKE ME...

I-I DON'T DISLIKE THEM, THOUGH.
IT'S JUST...

It's against the law to keep monsters as pets.
I-I KNOW THAT!

I KNOW...
怪獣保護
特区
許可無く
立入を禁
SIGN: MONSTER SHELTER DISTRICT / NO ENTRY WITHOUT PERMISSION
HERE IT IS.

WHAT DO WE DO? WE CAN'T GET IN.

PI (BEEP)

SHA (PSH)

I'M REGISTERED AS A MONSTER RESEARCHER AFTER ALL.

OH...

LOOKING CLOSELY, THERE'S QUITE A LOT OF THEM LIVING HERE.
MOST NON-FLYING MONSTERS NOT YET CERTIFIED AS "CLASS A" COME HERE.

IT LOOKS EASY TO GET HERE, BUT...

...IT'S CAMOUFLAGED SO THAT IT LOOKS LIKE AN IMPENETRABLE CLIFF FROM THE OTHER SIDE.
MOREOVER, THIS BRIDGE IS ONLY BIG ENOUGH FOR HUMANS TO CROSS, SO THE LARGER MONSTERS CAN'T GET OUT.

GO HOME.

LET'S GO.

OKAY ...

YOU SEEM DOWN.
I-I'M NOT!

BUS: TATARA ACADEMY ENTRANCE

SIGN: TATARA GIRLS' ACADEMY DORM #1

TSUKIKO, YOU IN THERE?
I'M COMING IN.
J-JUST WAIT A SECOND...
ガチャ
GACHA (KACHAK)

I THINK SOMETHING I BOUGHT YESTERDAY ENDED UP IN YOUR STUFF.
N-NOW'S NOT A GOOD TIME...

WHAT ARE YOU DOING, TSUKIKO?

MEOW!

パ
PA (FLASH)
パ

ピッ
PI (FLICK)

GOOD MORNING, EVERY-ONE.
WE ARE EXPERIENC-ING SOME TROUBLE, BUT LET'S PUT THAT ASIDE FOR NOW AND PRESS ON WITH OUR STUDIES.

SEEING AS YOU ALL INTEND TO BECOME TAMERS, SOMETHING LIKE THIS SHOULDN'T BOTHER YOU.

CHAPTER FOUR THE SILENT VISITOR
NOW THEN, LET'S BEGIN CLASS.

PICKED IT UP IN TOWN...?

THAT MON-STER?

YES ...

職員室

SIGN: FACULTY OFFICE

I'M SORRY.

I'VE FAILED YOU AS THE CHAIR OF THE TAMERS COMMIT-TEE.

SO EVEN YOU HAVE A SOFTER SIDE.
I'M ACTUALLY RLIEVED.

NO WORRIES. I'LL TAKE IT FROM HERE.

SUGITA-SENSEI ...
GARA (SLIDE)
'SCUSE US!

OH, THANKS FOR COMING, MY FIRST-YEAR TAMERS COMMITTEE MEMBERS.

SO WHAT DID YOU NEED US FOR?

WELL.
IT'S ABOUT THE MONSTER THAT'S ATTACHED ITSELF TO THE BUILDING SINCE THIS MORNING.

I'M LEAVING THAT TO YOU TWO.
PLEASE FIGURE SOME-THING OUT.
WHAT!?

SENSEI, YOU JUST SAID YOU WOULD TAKE IT FROM HERE...
I DIDN'T MEAN ME EXACTLY.
THERE'S NO WAY!

WHY NOT LEAVE IT TO THE HIGH SCHOOL TAMERS...?
WE TRIED THAT...

ZZZ
...BUT THEIR SKILLS ARE INTENDED TO CALM A RAGING MONSTER.
ON A MONSTER THAT'S ATTACHED ITSELF TO THE SIDE OF A BUILDING WHILE ASLEEP, THAT'S NOT GOING TO WORK.

THEN ...
...WE WON'T BE ANY MORE HELP THAN THEM...

WHAT ABOUT JUMBODON, THAT MONSTER YOU'VE BEEN CARING FOR?
MASTER OF THE FOREST
MAYBE BRING IT WITH YOU AND GET IT TO PEEL OFF THE OTHER ONE?

IS THAT KIND OF VIOLENCE OKAY?
HIS NAME ISN'T "JUMBODON," IT'S BLUE ...

ズシ
ZUN (THUD)
WE'RE COUNTING ON YOU, BLUE.

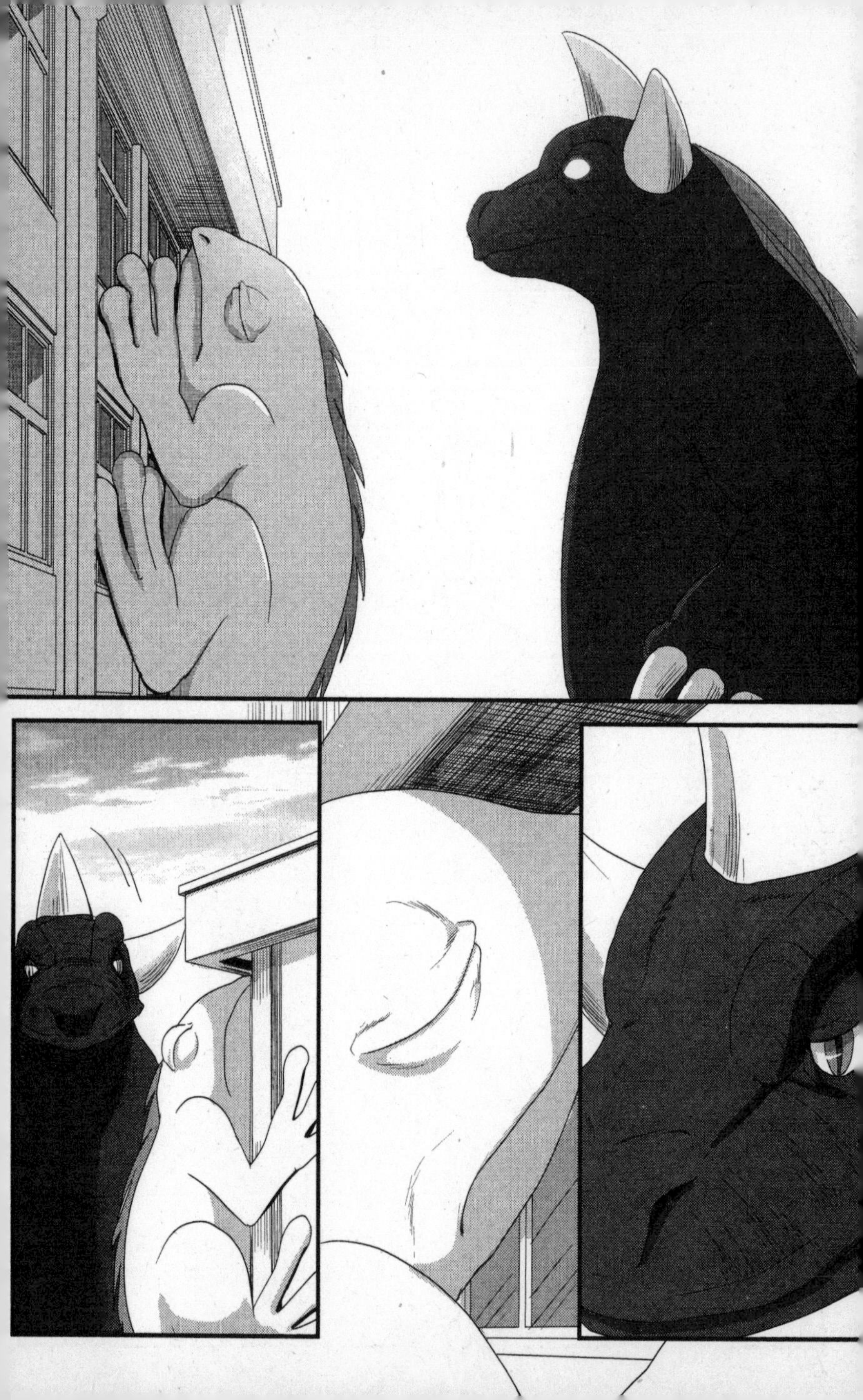

チチ…
CHICHI (CHEEP)
チチチ…
CHICHICHI

...NOW THEY'RE NAPPING WITH EACH OTHER.
THIS ISN'T GONNA WORK.

ざわ
ZAWA (CHATTER)
ざわ
ZAWA
ざわ
ZAWA

I THINK IT'S FINE AS IT IS.
THEY'RE NOT HURTING ANYONE.

BUT IT FEELS LIKE WE'RE TRAPPED IN HERE. I FEEL SO UNEASY.
IT WON'T TAKE LONG TO GET USED TO IT.

キーン
KIIN (DIIING)
コーン
KOON (DOOONG)
カーン
KAAAN (DAAANG)
HMM ...
ARE YOU THINKING UP SOME SORT OF STRATEGY, ION?
OH, UM... NO.
IF THINGS STAY AS THEY ARE...
...THEN I THINK MAYBE WE SHOULD... GIVE IT A NAME.
"LONELY CHAME-LEON."
THAT'S ITS NAME.

"LONE-LY"...?
"LONELY CHAME-LEON."

IT LOOKS LIKE A CHAMELEON, AND MORE IMPOR-TANTLY, IT'S LONESOME.

THAT'S TOO LONG.
WHY NOT SHORTEN IT TO "CHA-MELON"?
KOTO, YOU CAME.

JI (STARE)
じ

SHE'S FROM THE MONSTER RESEARCH LAB...
I THINK THE CHAIR SAID THEY'RE CHILD-HOOD FRIENDS.

THAT WON'T WORK. IT SOUNDS LIKE WHAT YOU WOULD NAME A TURTLE.
BUT CHAMELEON IS A LITTLE OFF TOO...
WHAT ABOUT "LONE-CHAN" OR SOME-THING?

ピキ
PIKI (CRRRK)
ピキッ
PIKI
ピキッ
PIKI

STONE
...?

BUT...

IF IT DIED AND TURNED TO STONE, THEN IT'LL BE EASY TO BUST IT UP AND DEMOLISH IT.
I'LL GO REPORT THIS TO SUGITA-SENSEI.

CHAIR-LADY!
ISN'T THAT A LITTLE...?

HEY, WAIT! CHAIR-LADY!

THAT MON-STER...

...REALLY TOOK A LIKING TO TSUKIKO.

IS IT...
...REALLY DEAD?
WHAT DO YOU MEAN...?
UM... WELL...
...I WAS THINKING ABOUT THIS WHEN WE SAW THOSE STONES BEFORE.

IT'S ALIVE?
WHO KNOWS...? THERE'S NOT MUCH OF A PRECEDENT FOR IT.
ON TOP OF THAT, THE PERSON WHO CHAMPIONED THE THEORY WAS RUN OUT OF THE ACADEMIC COMMUNITY.

ION HIDAKA.
WILL YOU PLEASE TRY SINGING TO IT?
HUH ...?

WH-WH-WH-WHY ME?
I HAVE SOME-THING I WANT TO CONFIRM.

YOUR SING-ING VOICE ...
...IS RATHER UNIQUE.

I-I DON'T REALLY UNDER-STAND.

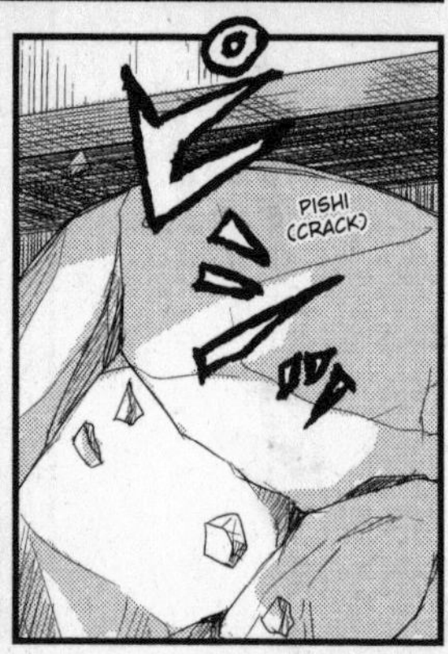
PISHI (CRACK)

HUH ...
KEEP GOING.

GARA (CLACK)

GARA
ガラ
GARA
ガラ
GARA
ガラ…

IT HATCHED ...
...ER, MORE LIKE IT TRANS-FORMED ...?

BIO-TORRENT ...
MIKIKO.
BASA (FLAP)
MAYBE THIS IS THE MISS-ING PIECE OF THE KAGU-RAZAKA THEORY.

YOU'RE ONE STEP CLOSER TO YOUR FATHER.

THAT'S ...
...NOT WHAT I WAS...

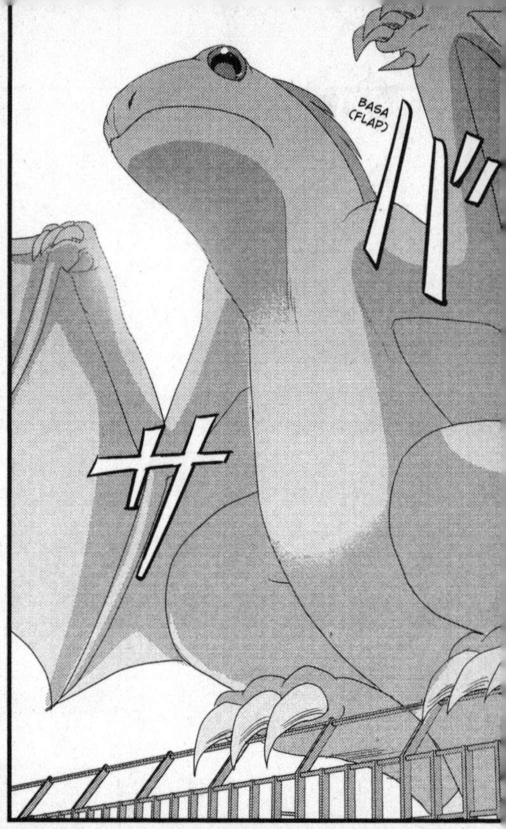
BASA (FLAP)

OH ...
IT'S GONNA TAKE OFF...

HUH ...?
ME ...?

KYU!

AND SO...

...THIS VISITOR WHO CAUSED SUCH A STIR LEFT (FOR HOME?).

CHAPTER FIVE THE GIRL AND THE MONSTER CHARMER

THERE WAS A PARK OUT-SIDE OF TOWN.
IT WAS ABANDONED, AND ITS PLAYGROUND HAD LONG FALLEN INTO DISREPAIR.
IT WASN'T A PLACE MANY PEOPLE VISITED.
WHEN I WAS LITTLE...
...I LIKED TO GO THERE AND SING BY MYSELF.
WHEN I SANG, THE TREES WOULD RUSTLE.
THE BIRDS WOULD GATHER AND JOIN IN THE CHORUS.
THE GRASS WOULD WAVE, EVEN THOUGH THERE WAS NO WIND.

ZA (ZSH)
NOW THAT I THINK ABOUT IT...
...I THINK I MIGHT'VE INADVERTENTLY CALLED IT...

EEEEEEK!

THAT CHILD TRIPPED TRYING TO ESCAPE!!
SUBE (SLIP)
ずべ
POLICE!
CALL THE POLICE!
NO, NOT THE POLICE. IT'S THE...WHAT ARE THEY CALLED?

IT'S ALL RIGHT...
DON'T BE AFRAID.

THAT OLDER TAMER GIRL...
...YOU MUST LOOK UP TO HER, ION.
YES, BUT...
...THINKING BACK ON IT, SHE MUST HAVE BEEN IN MIDDLE SCHOOL AT THE TIME...
SO SHE WAS PROBABLY A SENPAI OF OURS.
BUT THIS HAPPENED BEFORE I WAS EVEN IN ELEMENTARY SCHOOL.
SHE MAY BE IN THE UNIVERSITY.
WE ARE AN ESCALATOR SCHOOL AFTER ALL.
HUH.

OUR SCHOOL, TATARA GIRLS' ACADEMY, IS A MIDDLE SCHOOL, HIGH SCHOOL, AND UNIVERSITY ALL IN ONE.
IT'S A SCHOOL WITH A UNIQUE CURRICULUM FOR TRAINING SPECIALISTS, KNOWN AS "TAMERS," WHO MANAGE MONSTERS.

I, ION HIDAKA...

...AM A FIRST-YEAR MIDDLE SCHOOLER IN THE TAMERS PROGRAM.

ALONG WITH SORA MISUMARU, A STUDENT IN THE GEN ED PROGRAM WHO LOVES MONSTERS...
...WE'RE MEMBERS OF THE TAMERS COMMITTEE.

IF I REALLY EVER GOT TO MEET HER...
...I WOULD WANT TO GIVE A PROPER THANK-YOU.

SIGN: TATARA GIRLS' ACADEMY

IF I TOLD HER, "I BECAME A TAMER BECAUSE I LOOKED UP TO YOU"...

...I WONDER IF SHE'D CHEER ME ON.

多々良女学園

CHI (CHEEP) CHI...

CHI CHI CHI...

CHINMARI (SNUGGLE)

ちんまり

I KNOW IT'S SMALL, BUT IT'S THE BIGGEST ONE I HAD.
YOU'RE ALWAYS SLEEPING BY YOURSELF, BLUE, SO I THOUGHT IT MIGHT KEEP YOU COMPANY.

I GET IT, REALLY. IT KNOWS HOW YOU FEEL.
WELL, PROB-ABLY.
んぎゅ～～
NGYU~ (SQUEEZE)
I DON'T NEED YOU TO COMFORT ME!

キーン
KIIN (DIIING)
コーン
KOON (DOOONG)
AH, THE WARNING BELL.

ANYWAY, YOU AND BLUE ARE SO CLOSE.
IT'LL PROBABLY LOVE THAT CREEPY STUFFED ANIMAL.
DON'T CALL IT CREEPY!

HRM!

HUH?

IT'S SUGITA-SENSEI AND THE CHAIRLADY.

TRUCK: MONSTER TRANSPORT

怪獣運搬車

IT'S A STRANGE BREED, AND WAS JUST RESCUED FROM THE COAST THE OTHER DAY.

IT'S HUDDLED UP IN THIS TRANSPORT CAGE AND WON'T COME OUT.

I'M GOING TO TRY ONE MORE TIME.

Come on out, monster.

Right now.

Just open up that metal door.

Come on, come on, mon-ster—

I CAN'T PUT MY FEELINGS INTO IT IF I DON'T USE WORDS!
HIDAKA, I'M COUNTING ON YOU.

OH... OKAY.
HMM, I THINK WE LEARNED A SONG IN CLASS THAT MIGHT WORK FOR THIS...

TAMERS USE SONG TO CONVEY THEIR WILL TO MON-STERS.
THERE ARE A FEW MELODIES YOU CAN CHOOSE FROM BASED ON THE SITUATION.
APPAR-ENTLY, SKILLED TAMERS CAN EVEN IMPROVISE THEIR OWN SONGS.

ごそ…
GOSO (FIDGET)

IT MOVED.

SHURU (SLIDE)

ドスーン
DOSUN (PLOP)
シュル
SHURU (SLIDE)
YEEEEEEEEK!

OH, THAT'S NOT GOING TO WORK.
YOU CAN'T BE SO LOUD.

SAE-GUSA!
HEYA!
SUGITA-PAISEN, LONG TIME NO SEE!

YOU REALLY DID COME HERE FOR YOUR STUDENT TEACH-ING.
I THOUGHT YOU WANTING TO TEACH WAS SOME KIND OF JOKE.

HOW MEAN, PAISEN. AND HERE I CAME BACK BECAUSE I MISSED YOU SO.
YOU'RE SUCH A LIAR.
AND CALL ME SENPAI PROPERLY.

WHAT-EVER. YOUR TIMING IS PERFECT ANYWAY.
PLEASE TAKE THIS MONSTER TO THE HANGAR.
YOU'RE AS ROUGH WITH THE HELP AS EVER.

IT SEEMS TO BE ON EDGE, SO BE CARE-FUL.
OOH.

ガチャ
GACHA (KACHAK)
AH, HEY, DUMMY!

SHU (SLIDE
SAE-GUSA!!
GYU (TUG)

IT'S ALL RIGHT.
DON'T BE AFRAID.
WHA ...?

THE HANGAR OFF THE GYM WILL WORK, RIGHT?

DON'T YOU GIRLS GO IMITATING HER.

SHE'S A SPECIAL CASE.

SENSEI.

YOU DON'T MEAN SHE'S—

YEAH.

KYOUKO SAE-GUSA.
SHE'S THE "LAST MONSTER CHARMER."

ION?
たっ
TA (DASH)

UH...
UM!

SHU
(SLIDE)

BIKU
(JOLT)

YOU'RE ON THE TAMERS COMMIT-TEE.
YOU'RE AFRAID OF MON-STERS?

UH... UM.
WELL ...

WELL...IT DEPENDS ON THE MONSTER, I GUESS ...
BLUE... I MEAN THE MONSTER HERE AT THE SCHOOL, WE GET ALONG PRETTY WELL.

HRM...
AND YOU'RE TRYING TO BECOME A TAMER WITH THE WAY YOU ARE?

ARE YOU SURE YOU'RE SUITED FOR THIS?
WHY NOT GIVE UP?

CHAPTER SIX HEAVY BLOSSOM

I'M SAEGUSA.

STARTING TODAY, I'LL BE DOING MY STUDENT TEACHING HERE.

1-T

SAEGUSA-SENSEI IS A WORLD-CLASS TAMER.

HER TALENTS ARE SO UNMATCHED THAT SHE IS KNOWN AS THE "LAST MONSTER CHARMER."

SHE HAS RETURNED HERE TO HER ALMA MATER TO GUIDE YOU, HER UNDERCLASSMEN.

THIS ISN'T EASY...

FOR NOW, COULD I HAVE YOU STAND IN THE BACK AND OBSERVE THE CLASS?
SURE THING. THANKS.

ARE YOU SURE YOU'RE SUITED FOR THIS?
WHY NOT GIVE UP?

CHALKBOARD: ACADEMIC DEFINITION OF MONSTER BIOLOGY

怪獣の生物学的定義

WHILE WE GROUP THEM INTO ONE SPECIES, THERE ARE MAJOR DIFFERENCES IN SIZE AND FORM BETWEEN INDIVIDUAL CREATURES.

AND ONE CREATURE CAN HAVE A VARIETY OF FORMS.

THE MONSTER THIS MORNING HAD AN INTERESTING FORM.

I THINK IT WAS LIKE THIS...

HEY!
KUSU (GIGGLE)
くすっ

I WONDER WHAT WOULD BE A GOOD NAME ...

IS THAT THE MONSTER FROM EARLIER?
GATA (CLATTER)
ガタ

SIGN: FACULTY OFFICE

SEEING SCHOOL THROUGH A TEACHER'S EYES?
HMM.
YOU STILL DON'T SEEM TO BELIEVE I'M TRYING TO BECOME A TEACHER.
TRUE.
AWW.
IF YOU'RE SERIOUS, YOU SHOULD JOIN THE ADMINISTRATION.
YOU'RE JUST THE PERSON TO LEAD A GREATER COMMUNITY OF TAMERS.
I'M NOT GOOD AT MANAGING PEOPLE.
I'M BETTER OFF HERE BEING WORKED LIKE A DOG BY YOU, SUGITA-PAISEN.
THAT MAKES ME SOUND AWFUL. QUIT IT.

IT WAS SO MUCH FUN...

...BACK WHEN YOU AND I WERE ON THE TAMERS COMMITTEE.

IT MADE ME THINK IT WOULDN'T BE SO BAD TO TEACH HERE...

...WHERE I CAN TAKE CARE OF THE MONSTERS AT THE SAME TIME.

PAISEN, THAT'S THE THING ABOUT YOU...

...THAT DRIVES ME NUTS.

SO, WE'RE GOING TO GET SOME PRACTICAL EXPERIENCE.

THERE'S A MONSTER IN THIS PEN WE CALL THE "HANGAR" THAT WAS JUST BROUGHT IN THIS MORNING.
ゴオオオオオ
GOOOOO (SHOOOOM)

WE'RE GOING TO TRY CALLING IT TO US WITH THE SONG WE LEARNED THE OTHER DAY, MELODY #12, "INVITATION."
FIRST, ALLOW ME TO DEMONSTRATE.

WHAT IS THAT?

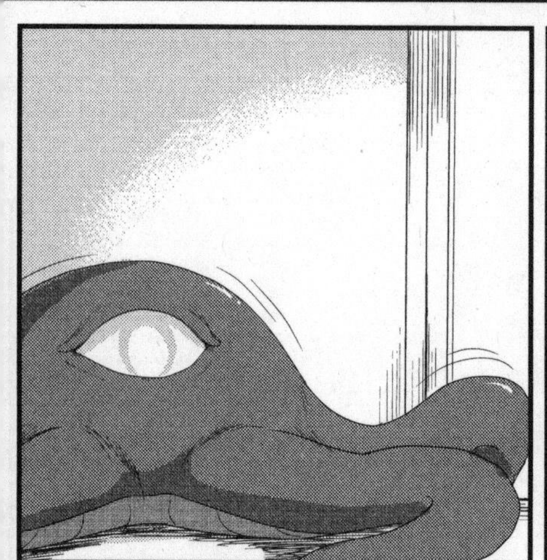

IT'S ALL RIGHT. IT'S A FAIRLY DOCILE MONSTER.
SOMEONE ELSE, PLEASE STEP FORWARD AND DO THE NEXT PART.

I DON'T THINK I'D SAY... DOCILE.
THIS MONSTER SEEMS UNWELL...

I WONDER...
...WHAT I SHOULD CALL IT.

ALL RIGHT, HIDAKA-SAN, GO AHEAD.

HUH ...?

WH... WHA—? I DIDN'T STEP FORWARD...

IT'S ALL RIGHT. IT'S YOUR FIRST TIME, SO IT DOESN'T HAVE TO BE PERFECT.

OH?

HIDAKA-SAN!!
DOSA (PLOP)

NOOO-OOOO!

ずーん
ZUUUN (GLOOOM)
IT'S NOT FUNNY, SORA-CHAN.
I'M SORRY, I'M SORRY.
I JUST WISH I COULD HAVE BEEN THERE.
MAYBE I'M...
... REALLY NOT MEANT FOR THIS.
ARE YOU STILL WORRIED ABOUT WHAT SAEGUSA-SENSEI SAID?
OF COURSE I AM.
ESPECIALLY AFTER SHE SAW ME LIKE THAT TODAY.
IT'S GETTING HARDER TO TALK ABOUT...
OH...

HUH ...!?
YO.

YES.
I WAS ON THE TAMERS COMMITTEE...
...SO THIS ONE AND I HAVE A LONG-STANDING RELATIONSHIP.
IT CAN BE VERY MOODY, HUH?

BUT IT'S GROWN VERY ATTACHED TO ION.
I-I GUESS SO.
I JUST FEEL LIKE IT SEES ME MORE AS A PLAYTHING...

THAT'S THE PROBLEM.
MONSTERS ARE ESPECIALLY SENSITIVE TO HUMAN FEAR.
IT'S HARD FOR THEM TO GET CLOSE TO SOMEONE WHO'S AFRAID OF THEM.

THOUGH, AT TODAY'S PRAC-TICE...
...THAT MONSTER SEEMED TO HAVE TAKEN A REAL SHINE TO YOU.

HUH ...

WHA-AAAA-!?
YOU WEREN'T EVEN AWARE ...

I THINK I GET IT.
YOU'RE AFRAID, BUT THEN YOU QUICKLY GET ATTACHED.
W-WAIT, I...

ION'S ALSO THE ONE WHO GAVE BLUE ITS NAME.
Y-YES, BUT...

IT'S PROBABLY ONLY A MATTER OF TIME BEFORE SHE NAMES THAT PRACTICE MONSTER TOO.
...I ALREADY DID.
ALREADY!?

"BLOSSOM" ...

...OR SOMETHING ALONG THOSE LINES...

HA HA AHH HA HA!

I'VE NEVER MET A TAMER QUITE LIKE YOU.

WH... WHAT ...?

WHAT'S WRONG, BLUE?

WHAT IS
THAT?

SUGITA-SENSEI!

WE'VE RECEIVED AN EMERGENCY COMMUNICATION FROM THE CITY.

職員室

SIGN: FACULTY OFFICE

AN ENORMOUS MONSTER HAS APPEARED IN THE OCEAN NEARBY.

IT'S RAPIDLY APPROACHING TATARA CITY.

IT'S COMING ...
CHAPTER SEVEN THE LONG AFTERNOON AT SCHOOL

SUGITA-SENSEI!

HAVE YOU FINISHED THE EVACUATION PROCEDURES?

YES, ANY STUDENTS STILL HERE AT THE SCHOOL HAVE TAKEN SHELTER IN THE GYM.

WHAT ABOUT THE ADMINISTRATION ...?

ZA (ZSH)

HUH ...?

THIS IS A MONSTER ...?

ZAPUN
(BLOOP)

SO MONSTERS CAN EVEN BE LIKE THIS.
IT'S AN ANOMALY—FUSED WITH SEAWATER INTO ONE FORM.

MELODY #5, "RETURN HOME."
THREE ...
NOW!

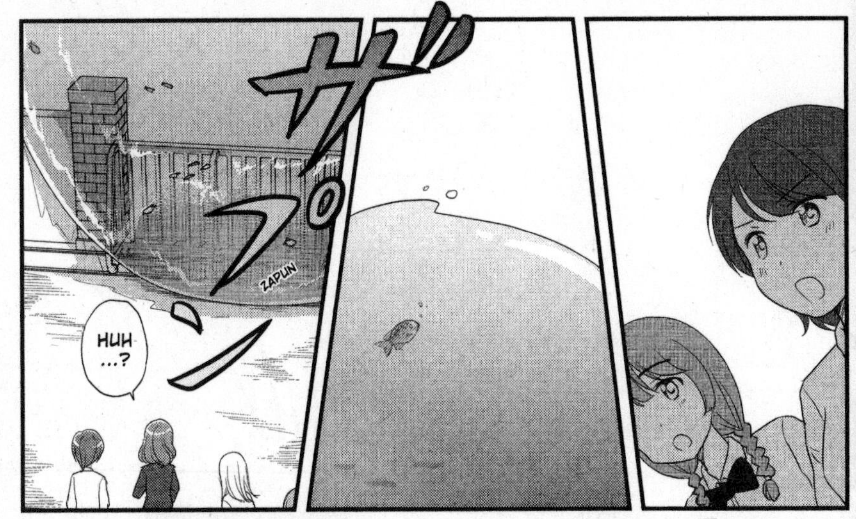
ZAPUN
HUH ...?

PLEASE TAKE COVER!
HEY!
WHY IS IT COMING CLOSER TO THE SCHOOL?

KAGU-RAZAKA.
MAYBE IT GOT SPLIT OFF FROM THE MAIN BODY.
DID YOU FIGURE SOME-THING OUT?
DOES ANYTHING COME TO MIND?

THAT MIGHT BE...
...A SATEL-LITE.

ZUN (THUD)
ZUN
PAI-SEEEN!
SAE-GUSA!
EVERY-ONE, PLEASE GET BACK.
THIS GUY'S GOING TO TRY AND PUSH IT BACK.
UH, JUST WAIT A SECOND.

ZABA
(BLOOP)
BASHA
(SPLASH)
IT WENT OUT THE OTHER SIDE!?
WELL... IT IS WATER.

OH NO!
IT'S GETTING FASTER ...
ZAZAZA (SWSHSWSHSWSH)
PAISEN !?

CAN'T SING...?
WHAT DO YOU MEAN, SAEGUSA?
IT SEEMS MY VOCAL CORDS HAVE GONE BAD.
THEY WEREN'T VERY STRONG TO BEGIN WITH, BUT THEN I PUT ALL THAT STRAIN ON THEM FOR YEARS.
MY DOCTOR SAID THAT...
...IF I KEEP SINGING, HE WON'T BE RESPONSIBLE FOR ME LOSING MY VOICE.
THAT'S WHY I...
...HAVE TO GIVE UP BEING A TAMER.

ピタ
PITA (PAUSE)
—THAT SINGING VOICE IS...

...GENTLE LIKE THE SEA, ACCEPTING EVERY-THING...

...STRONG LIKE THE EARTH THAT SUPPORTS ALL...

ANYWAY, IN ORDER TO STOP IT...

...WE'LL NEED STAROCTO OVER HERE.

HANAZONO-SENSEI AND THE HIGH SCHOOL TAMERS HAVE ALREADY HEADED FOR THE HANGAR.

HIDAKA-SAN, CAN YOU MEET UP WITH THEM THERE?

MISUMARU-SAN AND I WILL GUIDE STUDENTS AT THE GYM THROUGH THE EVACUATION.

THAT NAME.

BUT "BLOSSOM" IS SO CUTE.

HANAZONO-
SENSEI.

WHAT'S
GOING
ON?
THE
MONSTER
BECAME
GUARDED
AND WON'T
COME OUT.

HIDAKA-
SAN,
PLEASE
STAY
BACK.
IT'S
LIKELY TO
BEHAVE
AS IT DID
DURING
THE
HANDS-ON
PRACTICE.

AND YET...

HIDAKA-SAN!!

WHAT AM I DOING ...?

I'M SHAKING SO BADLY...

BUT...
...I UNDERSTAND.
BEING SEPARATED FROM YOUR BODY.
BEING BROUGHT TO THIS UNFAMILIAR PLACE.
THIS LITTLE ONE...
...IS PROBABLY MUCH MORE SCARED THAN I AM...
すぅ... SUU (INHALE)
IT'S ALL RIGHT. DON'T BE AFRAID.

BLOSSOM.
LET'S GO HOME.
HAHH...
ピチャ
PICHA (SPLISH)

!!
SAE-GUSA...!!
KOFF!
KOFF!
YURA (WOBBLE)
ゆら

HA HA...
GUESS I BETTER THROW IN THE TOWEL.

ドボーン
DOBON
(PLOP)

ザパーン
ZAPAAAN (BLAAAP)
ザザ…
ZAZA (ZSH-ZSH)
IT... RETURNED TO THE SEA?
...LOOKS LIKE IT.
SAE-GUSA-SENSEI!

CHICHI (CHEEP)
チチ
チチチ...
CHI CHI CHI
I SEE.
SO THAT LITTLE GIRL BACK THEN WAS YOU.
YES.
I'VE ALWAYS WANTED TO SAY THANK YOU FOR SAVING ME...
YET I WAS THE ONE WHO WRONGED YOU.

AH WELL.
HUH?
IT COULD BE SOMETHING OF A COWARD, SO I NEVER THOUGHT IT WOULD SHOW HIS FACE AROUND PEOPLE.
IT MUST HAVE REALLY LIKED YOU.

WHAAAAAT?
CHICHI (CHEEP)
CHICHI

SIDE STORY THE "FORMER" MONSTER TAMER GIRLS

MY BAD.

HEY, WAIT.

PASHI (WHAP)

IF YOU'VE GOT FREE TIME, THEN HELP ME.
IT'S TOO HARD TO SCRUB THIS GUY ALONE.

UH, NO.
HAVING ONE OR TWO PEOPLE WON'T MAKE A DIFFER-ENCE.
SERI-OUSLY.
GASHI (SCRUB)
GASHI

YOU'RE IN THE TAMERS PROGRAM, RIGHT?
YES.
WHAT ARE YOU DOING OUT HERE AT LUNCH?
NOTH-ING.

IT JUST... FEELS LIKE...
...I DON'T REALLY FIT IN ANY-WHERE.

YOU AREN'T AFRAID OF IT?
NO...

ONES THIS BIG ARE RARE.
A LOT OF STUDENTS ARE SO AFRAID, WE CAN'T GET MANY PEOPLE TO JOIN THE TAMERS COMMITTEE.

MY FATHER IS AN ADMINISTRATOR AT A MONSTER SHELTER DISTRICT.
I'VE BEEN VISITING THE SPECIAL DISTRICT AND PLAYING WITH MONSTERS SINCE I WAS REALLY LITTLE.
THAT'S PROBABLY WHY I'M NOT AS GOOD WITH PEOPLE.

NO!
THIS ONE IS REALLY KIND!
DON'T BE AFRAID!

YOU CAN'T PLAY WITH THAT LITTLE GIRL!
YOU COULD BE ATTACKED BY THAT MONSTER. IT'S DANGEROUS!

I THOUGHT THINGS WOULD CHANGE WHEN I CAME TO THIS SCHOOL.
BUT THAT HASN'T BEEN THE CASE AT ALL.
WELL THEN, STARTING TODAY ...
...MAKE THIS THE PLACE YOU FIT IN.

CAN I CALL YOU MY... PAISEN?

NO.

THANK YOU VERY MUCH FOR PICKING UP VOLUME 1 OF *MONSTER TAMER GIRLS*.

THE MONSTER IN THIS MANGA KNOWN AS "BLUE" IS BASICALLY "WHAT I THINK OF WHEN COMING UP WITH THE STRONGEST MONSTER." IT HAS THOSE THREE HORNS ON HIS HEAD AND LOOKS POWERFUL, RIGHT?

BUT IT'S ALMOST ALWAYS SLEEPING, AND EVEN WHEN IT DOES SOMETHING, IT'S NOT VERY HELPFUL...BUT I WANTED TO DRAW STRANGE MONSTERS LIKE THAT.

I THINK IT WOULD BE FINE IF THERE WERE JUST A MANGA ABOUT MIDDLE SCHOOL GIRLS WHO CARE ABOUT MONSTERS.

TO MY EDITOR, H-SAMA, WHO STUCK WITH ME FOR SUCH A STRANGE MANGA, THE *MANGA TIME KIRARA FORWARD* EDITORIAL DEPARTMENT, MY DESIGNER, AND TO ALL THE READERS WHO HAVE SUPPORTED ME SINCE THIS BEGAN PUBLICATION, ESPECIALLY THOSE WHO PICKED UP THIS BOOK...

...THANK YOU FROM THE BOTTOM OF MY HEART!

SHIMAZAKI MUJIRUSHI

Translation Notes

Page 34: **Gonsuke**, **Jumbodon** (*Dekaidon* in Japanese), and **Mountain Gori** are comically tough, masculine-sounding names in Japanese. *Gon* is also the name of a famous manga about a horned dinosaur.

MONSTER TAMER GIRLS

VOLUME 1

MUJIRUSHI SHIMAZAKI

Translation: AMBER TAMOSAITIS
Lettering: LORINA MAPA

Yen Press
1290 Avenue of the Americas
New York, NY 10104

Visit us at yenpress.com
facebook.com/yenpress
twitter.com/yenpress
yenpress.tumblr.com
instagram.com/yenpress

First Yen Press Edition: March 2018

Yen Press is an imprint of Yen Press, LLC.
The Yen Press name and logo are trademarks of Yen Press, LLC.

The publisher is not responsible for websites (or their content) that are not owned by the publisher.

Library of Congress Control Number: 2017963581

ISBNs: 978-0-316-51772-0 (paperback)
978-0-316-51773-7 (ebook)

10 9 8 7 6 5 4 3 2 1

WOR

Printed in the United States of America